Malta Tourist Guide

Attractions, Eating, Drinking, Shopping & Places To Stay

Stacy Lees

Copyright © 2015, Astute Press
All Rights Reserved.

No part of this publication may be reproduced, stored in a retrieval system, or transmitted, in any form or by any means without the prior written permission of the publisher, nor be otherwise circulated in any form of binding or cover other than that in which it is published and without similar condition being imposed on the subsequent purchaser.

If there are any errors or omissions in copyright acknowledgements the publisher will be pleased to insert the appropriate acknowledgement in any subsequent printing of this publication.

Although we have taken all reasonable care in researching this book we make no warranty about the accuracy or completeness of its content and disclaim all liability arising from its use.

Table of Contents

Welcome to Malta 6
Culture 11
Orientation 15
When to Visit 16
Recommended Sightseeing & Activities 18
   Valletta 18
      Valletta Living History 21
      National Museum of Fine Arts 22
      Grandmaster's Palace & State Rooms 24
      Scenic Seaplane Flight 25
   Saint Julian's 26
   Mdina 27
   Mnarja 28
   Sliema 29
   Tarxien Temples 30
   Malta's Carnival 30
   Hagar Qim Temple Complex 32
   Hypogeum Prehistoric Site 33
   Isle of MTV Music Festival 34
   Collegiate Church of the Immaculate Conception 34
   Vintage Bus Tour to Vittoriosa, Cospicua & Senglea 36
   Playmobil Fun Park & Factory 38
   Misrah Ghar il-Kbir Prehistoric Site 39
   St. Paul's Catacombs 41
   Gozo 42
      Azure Window 43
      Ta' Mena Estate & Agritourism 43
   Comino 45

Recommended Budget Accommodation 46
   Bohemia Villa & Garden (Boho) Hostel 46
   Corner Hostel Malta 47
   Hostel Malti 48
   NightCap Hostel 49
   Santa Martha Hostel 50

Recommended Budget Dining 50
- 1927 Restaurant 51
- Gululu 51
- Ir Rokna Restaurant & Pizzeria 52
- The Medina Restaurant 53
- Tre Angeli Restaurant 53

Recommended Shopping 54
- Bay Street Shopping 54
- Republic Street Shopping 55
- Ta'Qali Craft Centre 56
- The Point Shopping Mall 57
- Valletta Sunday Market 57

Welcome to Malta

Malta is a port-of-call on many Mediterranean cruises. The island attracts thousands of tourists annually with the beauty of its beaches and architecture as well as its impressive UNESCO World Heritage sites. The small Maltese archipelago of islands is located in the middle of the Mediterranean Sea, 50 miles south of Sicily. The three largest islands are Malta, Gozo, and Comino.

Malta gained its independence from the United Kingdom, in 1964 and is a member of the European Union. The Euro is the accepted currency.

Approximately 1.2 million tourists visit Malta each year and the country has two national languages, Maltese and English. Visitors from the European Union and the United States do not need to a visa for visits up to 90 days.

There are many contrasts on the island of Malta. Modern life and technology have seen apartment blocks spring up next to ancient temples. The good infrastructure that supports today's residents and visitors compliments the aging structures and hard-working lives of some of the rural Maltese people.

The island of Malta has everything that a visitor could want with luxury resorts and superb restaurants serving international cuisine, designer fashion shops and lively nightlife. The cosmopolitan atmosphere that prevails on Malta is less evident across the water on the island of Gozo. For a peaceful break we recommend you spend a few days on this tranquil island, perhaps staying in a traditional farmhouse, before heading to Malta.

The clubbing and nightlife centre of Malta is Paceville also known as PV. Paceville is located to the west of St. Julian's between Dragonara Point and Spinola Point. Named after Dr Giuseppe Pace who built the first modern houses in the 1920s and 1930s, the area took off when the Hilton and Sheraton hotel groups built five star hotels there thirty years later.

Over the years more bars, clubs, hotels and restaurants started to open to cater to the increasing numbers of tourists as well as the servicemen living in St. Andrew's, St. Julian's and Pembroke. In addition you will find a number of cinemas, gentlemen's clubs and casinos.

After a night out in Paceville many tourists head to the beach to relax, surf or windsurf under the Mediterranean sun.

The newer and busier resorts include Qawra and Bugibba on the north side of the island where some of the better beaches are to be found. The summer season is long on Malta and lasts well into October.

The most popular beaches are Golden Bay, Mellieħa Bay and Għajn Tuffieħa while Paradise Bay and Armier are smaller and quieter. Gozo and Comino offer clear water which is good for snorkelling. In Gozo the prettiest beach has red sand and is called Ramla l-Ħamra.

Just off the tiny island of Comino is the famous Blue Lagoon surrounded by gently sloping green fields, where the clear turquoise water shimmering over white sand will evoke images of the Caribbean.

If you are visiting Malta in August and fancy a night out with a difference reserve some tickets for the August Moon Ball. This glittering event has been held every year since 1958 at the Verdala Palace in Buskett and the proceeds go to the Malta Community Chest Fund. Around 1,000 people attend every year and dine under the stars in the palace grounds followed by dancing until the small hours.

Verdala Palace was built as a summer home for the Grandmasters of Malta and was designed by the same architect as the Grandmaster's Palace & State Rooms in Valletta. It is now used as in the summer by the President of Malta and his family. Tickets for the Moon Ball can be reserved at www.augustmoonball.com/

Malta has no less than nine UNESCO World Heritage Sites including the Megalithic Temples of Malta, Hal Saflieni Hypogeum, Victoria Lines and the Great Fault, the Grand Harbour and Valletta.

One of the island's attractions is the magnificent Mosta Dome. This huge church has the third largest unsupported dome in Europe and is dedicated to the Assumption. Taking 27 years to build, the designer was a Maltese architect, George Grognet de Vasse.

Malta is famous for its limestone but as de Vasse was not sure which quarry to use for his monumental structure he had stone samples from each sent to him in Mosta for testing. The stone he eventually chose came from near the old military airfield in Mosta at Ta' Vnezja.

The façade of the building is rather splendid in its own right but the actual dome-shaped roof is astonishing. The walls of the rotunda are nine metres thick and the dome has an internal diameter of 37 metres. The interior is stunning, with its many alcoves all beautifully and ornately decorated, surrounded by colourful paintings and frescoes. A row of arched windows runs round under the dome itself and allows the sunlight to flood in over row upon row of wooden chairs.

The Mosta Dome had a lucky escape during World War II when a 200lb bomb dropped by the Luftwaffe pierced the roof. Luckily for the 300-strong congregation the bomb didn't explode and a replica bomb is on display today.

For a typical Maltese snack look out for pastizz (pastizzi). These tasty local delicacies are available everywhere. The light and flaky filo pastry is typically diamond or round shaped and filled with mushy peas or ricotta cheese.

Two Guinness world records were obtained in Malta recently. One was for the biggest crowd of people dressed up as characters from storybooks; all 453 of them. The second record was for a 32 metre diameter Catherine wheel that was the largest in the world. The wheel was built by a firework factory in Mqabba and managed four revolutions under its own power. The record was awarded after a frustrating year for the firework factory as strong winds damaged the wheel and previous attempts had failed.

The Catherine wheel is named after the 4th century AD martyr Catherine of Alexander who was sentenced to death by "breaking on the wheel". The unfortunate victim's limbs were broken and then threaded through the wheel until the merciful release of death. However, the wheel broke when Catherine touched it and she was beheaded instead.

If you feel like hiring a car in Malta or Gozo driving is on the left as in the United Kingdom (it is humorously said that the Maltese drive neither on the left nor the right but in the shade.) Speed limits of 80 km/h on main roads and 50 km/h in built up areas often apply unless otherwise indicated.

Malta was classed as the 48th happiest country in the world according to a 2013 UN report.

Culture

The archipelago of Malta has just 415,000 residents. Due to its strategic location, the islands have experienced many different rulers from various nations and kingdoms. Greek, Italian, Arab, French, and British influences are still seen today. The Maltese language draws heavily from its Semitic roots, as well as from Italian, French, and English. It is unique as it is the only language that is still written in the Latin alphabet.

Malta has a long and colourful history and it is believed that the first settlers arrived from Sicily, some 100 km away. These first Neolithic people landed about 5200 BC and were mainly, hunters, farmers and fishermen.

In the following years they were joined by Phoenicians, Romans, Byzantines and Arabs until the early 16th century when the Ottoman Empire reached Malta. This led to one of the fiercest battles in the history of the island when Sultan Suleyman the Magnificent ordered an attack on the Knights of St. John.

This siege lasted several months through 1565 with 40,000 soldiers from the Ottoman Empire battling the 9,000 locals and a few hundred knights. Despite sending 200 ships with their men the Ottoman Empire was eventually defeated. The magnificent structures and defences built so long ago for the battle still stand proudly on the island today, many of them still intact.

The heavily Roman Catholic population has built over 360 churches on the three inhabitable islands with one church per 1,000 residents.

The Maltese are a generous people and the Charities Aid Foundation found in 2010 that about 83% of the population contributed to charity.

The locals are proud of the islands' cultural attractions including the nine UNESCO World Heritage sites and Malta's famous Caravaggio paintings which are displayed in the National Museum of Art.

The Maltese flag has two vertical stripes with white in the hoist and red on the fly. The only decoration on the flag is the George Cross. It is situated on the top left corner of the white part of the flag and was given by King George VI to Malta in April 1942 for bravery shown by the island's people during World War II. The people of Malta are patriotic and proud of their flag.

In addition to the Maltese national flag, a number of other flags adorn the tightly packed rooftops in the towns and villages. Expats often put up a flag from their home country as well as a local flag and it is easy to spot an impressive number of brightly coloured flags waving in the wind. Blue is popular and denotes the Blessed Virgin, Yellow is for the Pope and Red stands for the Republic.

The Maltese Cross was used by the Knights of Malta and can be seen everywhere and is available on many souvenir items.

The Maltese Luzzu are brightly painted boats which can be seen across the islands in the harbours and gently bobbing away at anchor. They are easy to spot with their double-ended hulls and bright colours of blue, yellow, red and green. On the bow you will often see a pair of painted eyes, a tradition derived from ancient Greek and Phoenician customs.

Some Luzzi are now used as tourist vessels but the majority as still used as fishing boats. The best place to see the colourful boats is in the harbour at Marsaxlokk. On a day when the sea has a calm mirror-like surface the Luzzi and their reflections offer some excellent photo opportunities.

Malta has two popular breeds of dog. The white coated and small Maltese Dog and the elegant and smooth-coated Pharaoh Hound. The Pharaoh Hound is sleek and agile with a powerful appearance. It is the national dog of Malta and occasionally used by Maltese men for hunting. In Maltese, the dog is called Kalb tal-Fenek which means rabbit dog. DNA tests have shown that there is no link to Egypt despite the name. Males grow to about 63cm and up to 25kg with females slightly smaller. An unusual trait of the Pharaoh Hound is its ability to blush. When the dog is happy or excited the nose and ears turn bright pink!

The tiny Maltese dog is believed to be one of the oldest dogs breeds in the world and references to it have been found as far back as 500 BC. It is sometimes called the Maltese Lion Dog and grows to a weight of about 4kg and 25cm tall.

A few superstitious beliefs prevail in areas such as pregnancy, childbirth, illness, and child rearing. One of these beliefs is called "il-quija". On a child's first birthday the parents surround the seated child with a variety of random objects. These can be a book, money, rosary beads or even a hard-boiled egg. Whichever object the child picks up first is supposed to be an indication of his or her future path. Money represents wealth and the book means the child will grow up to be a teacher. The egg is said to be an indication of fertility and the child will go onto to have a large family.

Not as commonly seen today is one of the ceremonies associated with death. The door knobs were removed from the doors of the dead, no cooking was allowed in the house and the men did not shave for three days. If the departed relative had animals a small part of its tail was chopped off as a sign of sorrow.

Malta is home to some rather unusual proverbs. For example:

"If a baby boy is born on the 15th August, the feast of the Assumption, he is likely to become a jockey."

"If a girl is born on a Friday at some point in her life she will be bitten by a dog on a Friday."

The Għajn or evil eye can be seen in many places on the islands. Not just as a symbol but as a malevolent look that is given by someone who wishes to curse another person. Many Maltese houses hang cow-horns on the walls to ward off evil or they will put a line of salt behind the front door to stop evil from entering.

One of the more inappropriate stories in Maltese folklore is the tale of the Gaw-Gaw. This slim, greyish man with a snail-like body patrols the streets sniffing out the breath of naughty boys. He would then slither in through a crack and grin at the unlucky child to scare them. Parents in Malta used to tell this tale to scare their children into behaving well. Another dubious tale involved the 'Tal-Ħabbgħażiż' man was said to put bad kids into a sack and take them away. 'Tal-Ħabbgħażiż' were the North African men who used to roam the street selling nuts and sweets.

Orientation

Malta's archipelago was formed by rising sea levels after the last Ice Age. Situated between the African and Eurasian tectonic plates, Malta is atop a shallow shelf with multiple natural bays and low hills.

Malta has very limited freshwater supplies. It is a country without mountains and there are no rivers and this makes it one of the world's ten worst countries for water supply per inhabitant. The natural supplies of water are limited and suffer greatly from the contaminants entering the aquifers. Malta produces nearly 60% of its water by desalination.

Despite the ideal location and vast potential for using natural power sources nearly all of the electricity on the island comes from oil and a 100% of the oil is imported.

In fact, nearly everything on the island is imported with only about 20% of the foodstuffs being grown on the island.

The economy of the islands depends heavily on income from tourists as well as financial services and limestone production. There is relatively low unemployment rate and a shortage of skilled workers. Poverty and social problems do exist in Malta but not on such a huge scale as many other countries in the EU. Young adults in Malta do not generally leave home until they get married as there is a limited amount of housing.

In the summer with the influx of tourists, the population triples from around 415,000 to 1.2 million. This results in a noticeable difference in the atmosphere on the island. Even out of the holiday season Malta has one of the highest densities in the world with 1,318 per square kilometre.

For an map of the Maltese islands see: http://en.wikipedia.org/w/index.php?title=File:EU-Malta.svg&page=1

When to Visit

Malta has a beautiful, subtropical-Mediterranean climate, making this a favorite tourist spot for international visitors. The winters are mild and summers are hot and dry.

January is the coldest month, but the temperature only drops to approximately 45 degrees Fahrenheit at night. The highs in August – the hottest month of the year – rarely hit triple digits. Instead, they average 90 degrees during the day and 70 degrees at night.

If you are looking to visit during the warmer months, plan your trip between mid-April and November.

Swimming in the ocean is pleasant from June to November, with the water temperature averaging 70 degrees.

Malta also has one of the highest numbers of sunshine hours in Europe and trips to Malta can be pleasant year-round.

Recommended Sightseeing & Activities

Valletta

Valletta is the capital of Malta and is located in the central-eastern portion of the main island. Due to the city first being constructed during the Order of St. John of Jerusalem, the architecture, style, and layout of the city is early-16th century Baroque with elements of Modern, Neo-Classical, and Mannerist styles in parts of the city. Many ancient and classical structures were lost during the Nazi air raids of World War II.

Cruise ships dock along the old seawall of the Valletta waterfront. The Forni Stores are also along the waterfront and are now shops, restaurants, and luxury stops during your trip.

Many of Malta's best cultural attractions are located in Valletta. The National Museum of Fine Arts is situated within a Rococo palace that dates back to the 1570s and formerly served as an official residence of the Commander-in-Chief of the British Mediterranean fleet.

The Manoel Theatre is the third-oldest working theatre in Europe and is the oldest working theatre in the Commonwealth of Nations. It is now Malta's National Theatre and was built in just ten months in 1731. It is now home to the Malta Philharmonic Orchestra. With 623 seats, the boxes are decorated with 22-carat gold leaf. Viennese chandeliers, a white Carrara marble staircase, and two water reservoirs create an outstanding acoustic environment, allowing for a remarkable experience throughout the show.

Roman Catholic and Protestant churches are located throughout the city, due to Malta's extensive religious background and heritage. Architecture fans will be impressed by the grand scale of Valletta's palaces. Many of them are still in active use, such as the former Palazzo Parisio (that now holds the Ministry of Commonwealth and Foreign Affairs) or the palace that is the current home of the National Museum of Fine Arts. The palaces are beautiful structures to see.

This Museum of Fine Arts houses works of art that were previously displayed in other palaces and churches throughout the nation. Many paintings and sculptures are now on display for visitors.

Military enthusiasts can visit the Grandmaster's Palace Armory Museum, which has a marvelous collection of suits of armour, arms, and guns that date back to the 15th century. The weapons and armour from the Renaissance era are unique compared to other eras. The museum has displays of armour from Spanish, French, Italian, and German backgrounds.

The National War Museum is located in Fort Saint Elmo and it reopened in 2008. Fort Saint Elmo has seen some intense fighting throughout the years, especially during the Ottoman Siege of Malta in 1565.

It memorializes Malta's suffering during World War II and the building's original purpose was as a powder magazine. There are many World War II relics within the museum, including an illuminated scroll from President Franklin D. Roosevelt that was given in 1943 to the "People and Defenders of Malta."

Valletta's National Museum of Archaeology is located inside the Auberge de Provence. This former palace displays Neolithic artifacts such as those found in the excavations of the Megalithic Temples of Malta, particularly the Sleeping Lady, Fat lady, and Venus of Hagar Qim.

If you are traveling with children you can occupy them at the Toy Museum. This museum has a collection of Corgi, Dinky, and Matchbox cars as well as toys from Malta and other countries around the world.

Across Valletta you will see watchtowers throughout the city that were built by the Knights.

Stop by one of the many cafés near the Triton Fountain. The fountain is surrounded by a number of statues that were constructed in 1959 and modeled in Classical and Baroque styles.

Valletta is a remarkable city with a varied history and many options for the modern traveler. The hotels can be slightly more expensive than in surrounding cities and towns, but the city is close to the main museums, palaces, and other sites you will want to see on your trip to Malta.

Valletta Living History

Embassy Complex, St. Lucia Street,
Valletta 1185, Malta
Tel: + 356 2722 0071
www.maltaattraction.com/

The Living History is one of the leading attractions of Malta and takes you back through time to discover the incredible past of Valletta. It shows how the first settlers arrived on the island and how Malta played its part in World War II. Malta has a rich and varied history and this 35 minute story is an excellent way of learning about the city before you go exploring.

The Valletta Living History film takes place in the state-of-the-art cinema right in the centre of Valletta, Malta's own UNESCO World Heritage city. Within the cinema complex there are also shops, restaurants and a games arcade.

The film is shown every day at 10:00, 10:45, 11:30, 12:15, 13:00, 13:45, 14:30 and 15:15 and the commentary is in English as well as seven other languages. An adult ticket is €10 and children pay €4. There is a family ticket for two adults and two children under the age of 13 which costs €25 available on the day or book online to get discounts.

National Museum of Fine Arts

South St. Valletta 1101
Malta
Tel: +356 2195 4341
www.heritagemalta.org/

The National Museum of Fine Arts is housed in one of the oldest buildings in Valletta which was originally built to house the Knights of the Order of St. John. In the early nineteenth century the palace was home to Comte de Beaujolais and then was named as Admiralty House in the 1820s. Famous residents and guests have included Queen Elizabeth II, Lord Mountbatten, Winston Churchill and George V. It remained in use as Admiralty House until 1974 when it became the most important art museum in Malta.

The High Baroque staircase as you enter the museum is impressive and one of the most important on the island. The two magnificent flights of steps are covered with elaborate sculptures and the many balustrades are equally as decorative.

Visitors can see collections of Maltese silverware as well as beautiful items of furniture, majolica pieces and paintings by local and internationally acclaimed artists. In the Green Room the gold-framed paintings are shown particularly well against the deep green walls complemented by highly polished pieces of fine wooden furniture.

There is a display of works by Mattia Preti, an Italian Baroque painter, which are the largest collection of his works anywhere on public display.

The museum holds many book presentations and lectures and has a very active programme of temporary exhibitions. The area of Valletta that the museum is located in is known for its many bars and cafès and the grid like streets that visitor usually explore on their way to or from the museum.

The National Museum of Fine Arts is open Monday to Sunday from 9am to 5pm with the last admission at 4.30pm. Adults pay €5 and there are reductions for students, senior citizens and children.

Grandmaster's Palace & State Rooms

Triq Ir-Repubblika
Il-Belt Valletta 1191
Malta
Tel: +356 2124 9349

The Grandmaster's Palace dominates the Palace Square and was one of the first buildings to be constructed in Valletta. Construction started in 1571 after it was designed by Gelormmu Cassar. The building has been extended and redeveloped by subsequent Grandmaster's over the years.

The palace has always hosted the government in Malta and is the site of the President's Office and the House of Representatives. When Malta was under British rule it served as the Governor's Palace. The Grandmaster's Palace and State Rooms are constructed around two courtyards, one of which is home to a statue of Neptune.

Inside the Palace, the Council Chamber is decorated with priceless tapestries with scenes from the Caribbean, Africa, South America, and India. These Gobelins tapestries were woven in France and are well preserved given their age of almost 300 years.

All of the rooms and passageways in the Palace are furnished with splendid artefacts and armour. The Palace Armoury is worth a visit and it is hard to imagine how anyone could have fought whilst wearing one of the heavy suits on display.

The Throne Room is stunning with intricate frescoes depicting the Great Siege of Malta while in the Hall of the Ambassadors visitors can see portraits of the Grandmasters. The Hall is also known as the Red Room and is decorated in rich shades of crimson with Louis XV furniture and an elaborate fresco detailing the history of the order of St. John.

Opening times are Monday to Friday 10am to 4pm and Saturday and Sunday 9pm to 5pm. The Palace is closed all day Thursday while the Armoury is open daily from 9am to 5pm. The entry fee is €5 for the Palace and €5 for the Armoury.

Scenic Seaplane Flight

Harbour Air Seaplanes,
Upper Vault 2
Pinto Wharf
Valletta (Waterfront)
Tel: +356 2122 8302

An exciting and different way to see the beauty of Malta and the neighbouring islands is to take a tour by seaplane. This exhilarating trip starts from the Grand Harbour in Valletta where you board the seaplane and take off across the waves and up to a cruising altitude of around 1000 metres.

It is a great way to see the Maltese archipelago and the famous sights of places like Mdina Cathedral, The Three Cities and the cart ruts at Misrah Ghar il-Kbir spread out below you.

The flight takes you across Malta in a northwesterly direction to the furthest tip of Gozo, a distance of about 35 kilometres.

As you turn back you might be able to catch a glimpse of Fungus Rock and the Azure Window on Gozo before heading back to Valletta and the Grand Harbour. Look out for the crystal clear turquoise waters of the beautiful Blue Lagoon as you fly over the island of Comino sandwiched between the two main islands.

The single engine Otter seaplane seats up to 14 passengers and has specially designed bubble windows so that everyone can make the most of the views and take some memorable photos. The cost of the tour is around €70/person and for an extra charge there is one seat available up front next to the pilot for a really special view.

The seaplanes take off and land from the Grand Harbour in Malta several times a day throughout the week. There is also a daily scheduled service between Malta and Gozo that takes around 15-20 minutes. The cost of a return ticket for adults is €80 and for children aged 3-11 the price is €61.

Saint Julian's

Saint Julian's is one of the best-known areas in Malta and is one of the most popular with active visitors. There are ways to stay within budget yet party like you are a celebrity. This party-oriented destination is located next to Sliema and is popular with young travelers and backpackers.

The patron saint of the city was known as Julian the Poor and Julian the Hospitaller and he became the patron saint of hunters. His feast day is celebrated annually on February 12.

The Spinola Palace, originally built in 1688, embraces its Latin architecture and provides visitors and residents with an impressive view as they walk or bike throughout the city.

There are public gardens within the city and al fresco dining is available along the Spinola Bay. At night, the atmosphere changes and the nearby nightclubs become active. The clubbing district of Paceville sees visitors and barhoppers in action. Some hostels and hotels offer organized bar crawls for guests. This keeps things safer, fun, and ensures people do not get lost by the end of the night.

If you prefer to enjoy St Julian's away from the hustle and bustle of the heavy partiers, take a stroll along the Promenade to Balluta Bay.

Mdina

This former capital of Malta is at the center of the island in a medieval-walled city. Called the "Silent City", Mdina has a population of only 300 people. Despite its tiny size, the ancient city still holds many architectural, historical and cultural wonders.

Visit the Mdina Dungeons located directly beneath the Magisterial Vilhena Palace. The underground passageways lead to chambers and cells that formerly saw much despair. Life-size figures help visitors to visualize the events from long ago.

Mnarja

Mnarja is celebrated each year on June 29th on the feast of St. Peter and St. Paul. This originated back in the 15th century and is still held today. The knights of St. John were the ones who originally declared June 29th as Mnarja, and initially named it "luminaria." There was a torchlight procession to the cathedral and the entire feast was first held at the grotto of St. Paul.

Later, the Maltese citizens began the celebrations at the Cathedral. Crowds continued to grow larger and are now filled with festive people singing, feasting, and enjoying the increasingly impressive activities. Fireworks can often be seen and the weather is typically pleasant which encourages outside activities.

If you will be in Nadur and Gozo on June 29th, stroll down the streets to see the decorations, excitement, and countless souvenirs and collectables devoted to Mnarja.

The Mnarja celebration is a wonderful experience to see during a summer trip to Malta.

Sliema

This city on the northeast coast of Malta has a bustling culinary, shopping, and tourist-driven culture. Formerly a sleepy fishing village, Sliema is home to beautiful churches that host popular feasts throughout the year.

The Roman Catholic religion is popular in Malta and Sliema has churches and cathedrals, notably, Our Lady of the Sacred Heart, St. Gregory the Great, Our Lady of Mount Carmel, and Stella Maris (the oldest parish church in Sliema and Gzira) among others.

Sliema hosts parish feasts throughout the year. Our Lady of the Sacred Heart and Our Lady of Mount Carmel feasts are both held in July. August will see the Our Lady of Stella Maris, while the feast of St. Gregory is celebrated in September.

If you would like to stay in Silema and take day trips to see the other sights in Malta, a ferry transports visitors to and from Valletta each day.

Cafés and shops are sprinkled throughout the city, where tourists and locals can enjoy traditional hospitality outside in the typically nice weather.

Sliema adjoins Saint Julian's and it is quite easy to visit both on a day trip. Due to its proximity to the bay, certified diving and snorkeling tours are available.

Tarxien Temples

Triq It Tempji Neolitici,
Ħal Tarxien 1063, Malta
Phone: +356 2169 5578

The Tarxien Temples are a part of the Megalithic Temples of Malta and were built in 3150 BC. The Tarxien Temples are three attached structures. They are mostly intact, with some of the more highly decorated slabs on display in the Museum of Archaeology in Valletta. In accordance with the other megalithic temples across Malta, the Tarxien Temples are composed of multiple apses. However, the middle temple has three apses instead of the normal two. One of the major attractions of these temples is the intricate stonework, including the reliefs of animals and other artistic patterns. Many of the Megalithic Temples involved animal sacrifices and the Tarxien Temples were no different. However, there has been no evidence discovered of ancient human sacrifices.

The Tarxien Temples and all Megalithic Temples of Malta have contributed to the significance of Malta as an ancient civilization. Although most of the artifacts are now housed at the National Museum of Archaeology - such as the famous Fat Lady - the structures themselves are a testament to the ingenuity of the ancient civilizations of Malta.

Malta's Carnival

The Maltese Carnival is held during the week prior to Ash Wednesday since 1535 when it was introduced by the Grandmaster, Piero de Ponte.

Common to the traditions of other carnival celebrations across the world, the Maltese Carnival incorporates parades, lavish costumes, fancy dresses, and a mask competition.

Masked balls are held throughout the week and the parade participants create colorful floats to the delight of audience members along the street parades.

This celebration has been a mainstay of Maltese culture for the past five centuries despite its scandal-ridden early years. King Carnival presides over the revellers, marching bands, and floats. The largest carnival celebrations are held in the capital, Valletta and in Floriana. Some of the smaller towns hold celebrations as well.

If you are looking for a more risque, less traditional Carnival experience, the Nadur Carnival exhibits cross-dressing, scantily clad clergy members and political figures and ghost costumes. The traditional dance of parata is a lighthearted reenactment of the victory over the Turks in 1565.

Other traditional dances are held during the events with mountains of traditional food available. Popular foods eaten at the carnivals include sugared almonds, perlini and prinjolata. This tall concoction of biscuits, almonds, citrus fruit and sponge cake is topped with cream and pine nuts.

Hagar Qim Temple Complex

Hagar Qim St,
Qrendi 2501, Malta
Phone: +356 2142 4231

The Hagar Qim temple complex is part of the Megalithic Temples of Malta. This unique religious monument dates from Ggantija times (3600-3200 BC).

Many rituals were performed in these temples including animal sacrifices, ritual oracles, and burnt offerings. Recesses exist in some areas of the structures indicating these activities by the archaeologists who excavated the site. Statuettes of deities and intricately decorated pottery were found while excavating the area, yet no evidence of burials. Its basic architectural design is similar to the other Megalithic Temples with the surrounding fortress and multiple apses composing the main and smaller buildings.

A visitors' center is available with an audio-visual introduction in the auditorium that you can view prior to the tour. An exhibition space displays several of the archaeological artifacts found in the temple as well as reproductions of damaged, destroyed, or alternately located artifacts. Most of the reproductions are currently in the Museum of Archaeology.

Hypogeum Prehistoric Site

Paola, Malta
Phone: +356 2180 5018

The Hypogeum is the oldest example of a prehistoric, underground cavity in Malta. It is a unique monument of rock-cut chambers, halls, and passages. It was rediscovered in 1902.

Historians believe the Hypogeum was first constructed around 3600 BC when builders began the upper level. The middle level was built between 3300 - 3000 BC and the lower level was finished between 3150 - 2500 BC.

The Hypogeum is one of the UNESCO World Heritage sites in Malta and is closely regulated by Heritage Malta to preserve its chambers, deposits, and paintings on the walls. Archaeological materials including pottery, amulets, figurines, and human bones were excavated from the site.

Only 80 people are allowed to visit per day so it is vital to call and reserve your spot as soon as possible. Sometimes tickets are available at the Museum of Fine Arts, but the tours fill up quickly.

Isle of MTV Music Festival

The Granaries
Fuq il-Fosos,
Floriana, Malta
Phone: +356 21235523
http://www.isleofmtv.com

This one-day free music festival is organized and broadcast annually by MTV and held in the Granaries in Floriana. Some of the most well known musicians who have performed in the past include Black Eyed Peas, Lady Gaga, Snoop Dogg and Flo Rida.

Since 2008, the Isle of MTV has become a huge free music festival and party location that attracts audiences from around Europe. Attendance is on a first-come, first-serve basis so get in early. The festival is usually held during the last week of June and the line-up is announced in March-April.

Collegiate Church of the Immaculate Conception

65, Triq il-Gendus,
Bormla, BML 1025, Malta
Tel: +356 2182 8413
www.thechurchinmalta.org/

Malta and Gozo only cover a small area but between them they have an impressive 359 churches, with 313 in Malta and the rest in Gozo.

This equates to slightly over one church per square kilometre. Some of the localities have more than one parish church with Sliema and Birkirjara having four each.

The Collegiate Church of the Immaculate Conception is in the Cospicua area of Malta and is the largest monumental building in the area. The first church on the site was built in 1584 and enlarged in 1637 and yet again in 1732 when it was completed and finally consecrated. The church stands on a hill and according to legend it is here that the Blessed Virgin appeared to save a small child from the clutches of the devil.

Somehow the church escaped undamaged through the bombings of World War II and now houses many exquisite works of art. One of its greatest treasures is a painting by the 17th century painter Polidoro Veneziano of Abruzzo. His painting of the Madonna and Child sits behind the high altar and is much admired by people the world over.

The statue of the Immaculate Conception that can be seen in the church is quite simply breathtaking and dates from 1689. The wooden statue is said to have been sculpted by a Carmelite nun. Not much of the original wood can be seen, only the head, hands and feet, as the statue was sent to Milan in 1905 to be covered in silver.

Inside the church are opulent treasures including silver candlesticks, the Missal and antependia and a diamond studded monstrance.

There are numerous altars and on feast days these are decorated with beautifully designed altar cloths embroidered with gold. The church celebrates its main feast day on December the 8th but the festivities start two weeks beforehand when the city becomes alive with brightly coloured bunting, noisy rockets and marching bands.

Mass is held several times a day all through the week with the earliest service being at 7am, and the last one at 6pm. Each day is different so check the website for times before visiting.

Vintage Bus Tour to Vittoriosa, Cospicua & Senglea

Supreme Travel,
Kastellan Road, Zejtun
ZTN 4400, Malta
Tel: +356 2169 4967
www.maltasightseeing.com/

Climb aboard a vintage bus for a tour of the Three Cities of Malta and be transported back in time. The vehicle used is one of the first wooden-bodied buses made by local mechanics and carpenters which were purchased in 1921 by the Cottonera Motor Bus Company.

The drive takes you to the fortress of Cottenera which houses the Three Cities of Vittoriosa, Cospicua and Senglea, all of which were built and then fortified by the Knights of Malta. Cospicua has been around since Neolithic times and up until the 18th century it was known as Bormla. The construction of the wall to safeguard the city was not started until 1638 and finished some 70 years later.

Vittoriosa has always been associated with the shipping and marine trades as it is ideally situated with safe anchorage. The significant position of Vittoriosa in the Grand Harbour meant that any military powers that wanted to rule Malta has to first take control of this city.

There are several of Malta's main tourist attractions in the Vittoriosa area. The Waterfront is where the former Palace of the General of the Galleys and Order of St. John's treasury were. Refurbished at the start of the new millennium the Palace is now a casino and the treasury is home to the Malta Maritime Museum. The Vittoriosa 1565 Museum is in the same area and tells the story of the battle and siege of the town in 1565.

The vintage bus tour continues onto Senglea which during the time of the Knights of St. John was joined by a bridge to Cospicua and is now peninsula in shape. Senglea was originally a hunting area and the first building was not constructed until 1311 when St. Julian's Chapel was founded. Fort St. Michael in Senglea took about a year to build and was completed in 1553 followed by the building of the walled town through the next decade.

The tour leaves at 11am and 2.30pm from Sliema Ferries Monday to Friday and at 11am only on Saturdays. The tour does not operate on Sundays or Public Holidays. An adult ticket for the two hour tour is €15 and children between 5-15 years pay €9. The commentary is in English and passengers can be picked up and dropped off at any Malta Hotel.

Playmobil Fun Park & Factory

HF80, Industrial Estate,
Hal Far, Birzebbuga 3000
Malta
Tel: +356 2224 2445
www.playmobilmalta.com/

Children love Playmobil figures and play-sets and this fun activity gives them the opportunity to play with as many as they want to. Many of the figures are life-sized even the Playmobil animals with horses that can be sat on for great photos. There are inside and outside play areas with different themes and activities according to age.

The huge sand pit has many of the children's favourite characters in and the water-based activities on the lake include rope bridges and log rafts as well as a Playmobil pirate ship that landlubbers can go aboard.

There is a cafeteria for hungry adventurers, and their parents, where a good range of snacks and meals can be bought at reasonable prices. There are organised craft workshops as well, usually at weekends and school holidays where children can take part in face-painting, pottery and similar activities.

At the Playmobil FunPark shop there are lots of exciting souvenirs of the day and if you need some spare parts for a toy back home the staff will be happy to help. For any one that wants to see more of the Playmobil Factory and see how the smiling faces of the figures are brought to life there is a guided tour that last 45 minutes. It is recommended to call and reserve a place in advance.

The Playmobil FunPark is open all year round Monday to Sunday from 10am to 6pm. Adults pay just €1.20 to get in and admission for them is free after 1pm as long it is not a weekend, public holiday or school holiday. Children between 1-12 years pay €2.40 all day.

Misrah Ghar il-Kbir Prehistoric Site

Dingli Cliffs
Siggiewi, Malta
www.cartrutsmalta.com/

This prehistoric site is most famous for its complex network of cart ruts gouged into the rock. There has been a lot of speculation as to the reason for the ruts without a definite answer. Most archaeologists think the site was developed around 2000 BC at the start of the Bronze Age in Malta when settlers came to Malta from Sicily. Some theories suggest that the ruts were caused by wooden wheels of carts eroding the soft limestone or by sledges transporting goods or that it is a primitive irrigation system.

There are several sites with these ruts in Malta and Gozo but the best are here in the southwest of Malta near Dingli Cliffs. The area is the size of several football pitches. Other ruts have been found that appear to go straight off the edge of the cliffs and ruts have also been found on the seabed.

The Dingli site is informally known as Clapham Junction after an Englishman was reported as saying the ruts reminded him of this train station in London, England. Indeed the cart ruts do look like they should be a system of railway tracks. Some run parallel and some crossover giving the impression of junctions. Many of the ruts are up to 60cm deep and the parallel lines have distances of anywhere from 110cm to 140 cm between them. Along with the ruts there are definite shapes of triangles, squares and rectangles that are clearly visible made from lines of rock.

Ghar il-Kbir is Maltese for Great Cave and at the site there is a large crater in the ground that has a series of smaller caves at the sides where the Troglodytes used to live. Many of the cart ruts lead right to the entrance of the Great Cave.

The site at Misrah Ghar il-Kbir is an open site; therefore there are no opening or closing times and no entrance fee. There are no facilities at the site so if you are visiting in the heat of the summer take plenty of water and something to cover up with in the sun. There is very little shade unless you go into the Great Cave.

The cart ruts are quite a distance from Dingli although this is where they are said to be. The closest bus stop is about 500 metres away at Buskett.

St. Paul's Catacombs

St. Agatha Street,
Rabat, Malta
Tel: +356 22954000
www.heritagemalta.org/

The catacombs that are open to the public are only a tiny part of the extensive network of underground tombs and galleries that date from the fourth to the ninth centuries. In 1894 Dr Antonio Annetto Caruana made a full investigation of the site which is now managed by the Heritage of Malta.

The complex consists of two parts; St. Paul's and St. Agatha's. St. Paul's is part of large cemetery that was outside of the city walls of Melite, an ancient Greek city, which is now covered by Rabat and Mdina. Within St. Paul's is St. Agatha's, San Katald, St. Augustine and many others.

The catacombs were dug outside of the city walls not just for hygiene reasons but so there was room for mourners to congregate and elaborate burial rituals could be performed. At the end of one of the tunnels the Agape table can be seen. This is where the ritual meals where held in celebration of the life of the departed relative.

Any remains or contents of the tombs have long since gone although very occasionally a bone is stumbled on. Different types of tombs can be explored including baldacchino tombs, window tombs and locúli tombs. In some of the window tombs it is possible to see the purposely carved indentations where the head of the deceased would have rested.

Visitors are allowed into two of the 24 catacombs in the St. Paul's complex. As you descend the steps between the living world and the world of the dead it is hard not to feel a sense of awe. Not just the fact that so many people were laid to rest under Mdina but the work that went into creating this complicated and intricate network of catacombs that cover around 2000 square metres. The steps lead down into large halls with pillars in the style of Doric columns and which would have had many painted and decorated plaster objects on. These have long since disappeared.

The catacombs can be visited Monday to Sunday from 9am to 5pm, the last admission is at 4.30pm. An adult ticket costs €5, children pay €2.50 and students and senior citizens pay €3.50.

Gozo

This is the second largest island of the Maltese archipelago. Fishing, crafts, and agriculture are popular on the island which also includes the Ramla I Hamra beach with its red sand.

Every year in mid-autumn, the island hosts a Festival Mediterranea with outdoor live music, tours around historic and ancient spots, events centered around food and drink, and art exhibitions. In order to add an educational aspect to the festival, seminars and field trips are often held.

Azure Window

Inland Sea & Dwejra Bay, Gozo

This stunning natural arch is located on the island of Gozo near to the Inland Sea and Dwejra Bay. Scuba diving enthusiasts can dive in this area and it is a popular site. Swimming and boating are also popular. Some have even jumped from the arch when cliff diving (this is illegal and dangerous). The Azure Window is disintegrating and pieces of rock continually fall into the ocean. It is a worthy site to visit now due to its likely disappearance in a few years. Once the arch crumbles away, it will be renamed the Azure Pinnacle instead of the Azure Window.

Ta' Mena Estate & Agritourism

Rabat Road, Xaghra, Gozo, XRA 9010
Tel: +356 2156 4939
www.tamena-gozo.com/

This is a unique venture into the world of agro-tourism where the natural surroundings have been utilised along with family traditions to produce excellent food and wine. Following the dream of their late mother the Spiteri family have spent seven years cultivating the 25 hectares of land into an agricultural project where visitors can not only buy the products but learn about the making of them as well.

The owner and his family are on hand to guide visitors around the estate and explain about the goats and other livestock and share their comprehensive knowledge about the products they grow. There are extensive olive and citrus orchards, vineyards, herb gardens and vegetable plots.

A lot of the foods available are preserved with the help of just the Mediterranean sun and marine salt, reflecting how many years ago people didn't have fridges and freezers to keep their foodstuffs in. There is a long list of foods preserved in this way such as Prickly Pear Liqueur, Sun Dried Tomatoes and Wild Capers in Vinegar. Visitors are encouraged to help with the picking of the fruits and vegetables and experience how these foods are preserved.

The Spiteri family say that they don't run a restaurant but there are often pizzas and other homemade goodies available to try. There is an excellent gift shop with a comprehensive range of all the goods produced on the Ta' Mena Estate. The estate produces several wines which are highly thought of across Malta, including table wines and the rather interestingly named Ancient Gods Range.

The Ta' Mena Estate is open from 9.30 until 5pm every day and it is free to walk around the estate with no pre-booking. Every Saturday at noon an organised tour of the estate takes place with a food and wine tasting session afterwards. The tour lasts about two hours and they ask that you book in advance for this.

Comino

The smallest of the islands, Comino is mostly uninhabited and has only one hotel. Located between Malta and Gozo, Comino is more of a nature reserve than a residence. This is a great spot to visit if you are looking for a quiet, serene vacation. The one policeman and one priest commute from Gozo to render services to its four permanent residents and the tourists who visit.

The St. Mary's Tower is the most visible structure on the island. Visitors taking a comfortable walk and appreciating the nature and bird sanctuaries will be able to see this building on the highest hill of the tiny island. The towers alternately served as an early warning system, prison, and now a staging post to guard against illegal hunting of migratory birds at sea. Due to its picturesque location, St. Mary's Tower has appeared in a number of films, most notably The Count of Monte Cristo.

Battle and military enthusiasts can visit St. Mary's Battery, originally constructed in 1716. Two 24-pound cannons are still inside the structure and were used to guard the island from any potential military invasions. It was recently restored in 1996, making this a safe, fascinating site to visit.

If you would like to stay on the small island and enjoy seclusion from the more crowded, interactive main island of Malta, there is just one hotel in Comino. Comino Hotel (San Niklaw Bay, Comino SPB08, Malta. Phone: +356 2152 9821) was constructed in 1960 and has two private beaches for its guests. The original location is above Saint Niklaw Bay. It also has private bungalows for the more private among us in Saint Marija Bay.

Recommended Budget Accommodation

Bohemia Villa & Garden (Boho) Hostel

Villa Cycas, Dun Guzeppi Xerri Str.
St. Julian's STJ10, Malta
+356 2765 6008
http://bohohostel.com/

If you are a young backpacker either traveling alone or in a small group, then Bohemia Villa and Garden (Boho) Hostel in St. Julian's may be a good place to stay.

They specifically request non-partiers so that the other residents are able to enjoy a peaceful stay while still making new friends from across the world.

Bohemia Villa and Garden is just ten minutes from Balluta Bay. Lockers, television, and breakfast (from September through May, not during the summer) are all included in the fee. Guests can rent towels.

There is no curfew, but hostel owners suggest that those looking to party stay at the Nightcap Hostel in the clubbing district. The beds book fast so plan in advance.

The rates vary based on the season, but beds in the dorm rooms are usually below €20 per person with a private room costing approximately €23-€25 per person per night.

Corner Hostel Malta

6, Saint Margaret Street
Sliema, SLM1979 Malta
+356 2780 2780
http://www.cornerhostelmalta.com/

This former townhouse renovated its rooms to offer both private and shared rooms to guests. Included with the room rates are free WiFi, fully equipped kitchen, linens and lockable storage. There is an additional cost for towels, but children are allowed if accompanied by an adult. Rates vary by season, but start around €20 for the mixed dorm, €22 for single sex rooms, and €25 for private rooms.

The hostel is very close to the beach, where visitors can see the cliff diving and tour the surrounding areas. A consistently highly ranked hostel, Corner Hostel encourages friendship among the guests with a communal kitchen and a common room. It is close to the many sites in Sliema, Malta.

Hostel Malti

41, Birkirkara Hill Ta Giorni,
St. Julians STJ 1147, Malta
+356 2730 2758
http://www.hostelmalti.com/en/home.htm

If you are looking for an affordable place to stay while traveling in Malta, the Hostel Malti is a great option. Its motto is "for the scruffy and happy backpacker."

Only allowing visitors 18 and up, this hostel has unique amenities such as a BBQ area, sun deck, and Jacuzzi as well as benefits that are provided by most hostels across the world. Bring your own towels, but linens and WiFi are included in the fee. Rates for all dorms start around €18. There is one all-female dorm and three co-ed dorms. The brightly colored hostel encourages friendship among its guests and has four themed dormitory rooms: sun, sea, surf, and sand. Quiet time begins after 11 p.m., but the staff organizes a pub-crawl most nights of the week for the party lover.

NightCap Hostel

Wilga Street, Paceville,
St. Julians, Malta
+356 2704 0030
http://www.nightcaphostel.com/

Parties and social animals visiting Malta will particularly enjoy NightCap Hostel. Located in the heart of the St. Julians clubbing district, this hostel caters towards those on holiday, students, and young adults who enjoy to party. This hostel offers multiple amenities in addition to its affordable rooms, including free WiFi, lockers, and kitchen facilities. There is no curfew or lockouts and towels are for rent. St. George's Bay is a mere two-minute walk away and multiple shopping centers are nearby in addition to restaurants, bars, and nightclubs.

The rooms are designed for maximum interaction with other travelers. There are mixed and single-sex dormitories available, all starting around €20 per person per night. The roof garden is equipped with couches, center tables and comfy chairs for socializing in the summer. Adults 18 and up only.

Santa Martha Hostel

Qolla Street, Marsalfom,
Gozo, Malta
+356 2155 1263
http://www.santamarthahostel.com/

This little family run hostel is located in Gozo and is just a five minutes walk from the beach. Gardens in the front and back lend to the charming façade. Rooms start at about €20 per person per night and there are single, double, or triple bedrooms. Breakfast is included or guests can store their own food and prepare it themselves. Gozo is one of the main islands in the archipelago and restaurants, bars, and bike rental shops are located nearby.

Recommended Budget Dining

Tipping is customary in Malta. It is reasonable to tip between 5% and 10%, depending on the quality of service provided.

1927 Restaurant

St. George's Road,
Saint Julian's, Malta
+356 2135 4361

The restaurant formerly known as Tal-Kazin Maltese Restaurant consistently receives good reviews from locals and visitors. The menu specials change on a daily basis depending on what is fresh or recently caught. The portions are large and great for a couple's night out or to share with friends. The intimate atmosphere lends itself for great conversation, flowing wine, and appreciation of great pasta, seafood and meats. Plan to stop for dinner before the sun goes down and request a table outside.

Gululu

133 Spinola Bay,
St. Julians, Malta
+356 2133 3431
http://www.gululu.com/mt

This traditional Maltese diner is found on the waterfront of Spinola Bay. Here, you can get traditional Maltese dishes like Torta tal-Fenek (rabbit pie), Aljotta (fish soup), and mize (a variation on the traditional eastern Mediterranean meze). The prices are moderate and what you would expect to find at a bay front restaurant.

However, with inside and outside seating and a casual atmosphere, it can be worth it to relax, take in the view, and enjoy some delicious Mediterranean-inspired and traditional Maltese food for either lunch or dinner.

Ir Rokna Restaurant & Pizzeria

Church Street, Paceville
Saint Julian's, STJ 3044, Malta
+356 2138 4060
http://www.rokna.com/

This family-run restaurant claims its status as the oldest pizzeria in Malta. It is located in the Rokna Hotel and offers at 10% discount to hotel guests. A family-friendly spot, Ir Rokna serves large portions at reasonable prices. There are many pizza options for under €15. Additional toppings include Maltese sausages, mussels, jalapenos, and Mozzarella di Bufala.

The restaurant offer grilled lamb, steak, pork, and various types of fish in addition to chicken and pasta choices. They offer a special kids menu with child-friendly portions.

Ir Rokna Restaurant and Pizzeria is a great place to enjoy dining in a comfortable atmosphere. They take reservations over the phone and deliver.

The Medina Restaurant

7 Holy Cross Street, Mdina, Malta
+356 21 45 4004
http://www.mol.net.mt/medina/

A romantic foodie destination in the middle of an 11th century Norman residence, the Medina Restaurant is the location for couples and adults who enjoy great food with a pleasant ambience. Al fresco dining is available year-round with a fire lit during the winter months. Take a walk before or after dinner in the narrow, lamp-lit streets of Mdina.

Mediterranean fare is the highlight here with generous portions of charcuterie (including braesola), mozzarella di bufalo, and portabello mushrooms. Mediterranean meats and fish are available, prepared in an array of sauces with a meticulous, final presentation.

Tre Angeli Restaurant

91 The Strand,
Sliema, SLM 1022 Malta
+356 2731 4753

Tre Angeli defines itself as a "modern twist of Italian and Maltese cuisine." The chefs offer Mediterranean, Russian, and Italian-style cuisine in addition to native Maltese dishes, such as rabbit, ravioli, or bragioli.

Traditional Maltese pastries are also available. This restaurant is open throughout the day for breakfast, lunch, dinner and late night snacks after your nighttime adventures.

There is outdoor seating to enjoy the breeze from the Mediterranean Sea. Locals and tourists frequent the restaurant, making it a great stop to mingle with an international population and enjoy good food and drinks.

Recommended Shopping

Note that some shops in Malta will close from 1:00 p.m. to 3:00 or 4:00 p.m. for siesta.

Bay Street Shopping

Bay Street, St. Georges' Bay,
St. Julian's, Malta STJ 3311
+356 2138 0601
http://www.baystreet.com/mt

If you are looking for a variety of items plus dining options and the occasional sale, stop by the Bay Street Shopping Center. This area of St. Julian's offers something for all ages and tastes. There is a Fun City Amusement Park on the second floor with arcade games, a soft play area for smaller children, children's rides, and a pool table.

For some pampering, visit the spa and rooftop pool bar. Women can go to Capellimania for beauty and hair services. Both sexes can book treatments at Beijing Rose. Unwind in the sauna before a Chinese massage or facial. Get manis and pedis, make-up applications, or even a body wax to prepare for that special night out.

Looking to bring home a unique, yet temporary souvenir? Stop by Henna Tattoo on Level 0 and choose from a variety of designs.

Bring your swimsuit and head to Level 7 for the 7th Heaven Rooftop Pool and a beautiful view of the St. George's Bay.

Check the website to see if specials and offers are available when you visit.

Republic Street Shopping

Valletta, Malta

Located in the heart of Valletta, Republic Street runs from Republic Square to Valletta's main gate. This pedestrian street market has shops that sell clothing, souvenirs, and handmade or hand-forged objects. The further down the street you go, the more affordable the products become.

Stop by the Silversmith's Shop at 218 Republic Street to watch the silversmith forge a necklace or pendant in front of you. Buy a Maltese Cross to remember your visit to the island.

Malta's proximity to mainland Italy leads to an abundance of quality Italian leather goods, particularly Italian leather shoes, on sale in various stores both here and around the peninsula.

Ta'Qali Craft Centre

Ta'Qali, Attard, Malta
+356 2291 5400
http://www.new.visitmalta.com/en/info/taqalicraftsvillage

The Ta'Qali crafts village is popular for visitors looking to buy handmade items. You can watch craftsmen blow glass to create an eight-pointed Maltese Cross as well as to decorate pottery pieces. The craftspeople also create and decorate knitwear, jewelry and ceramics as well as gold and silver products. Metalworkers work with bronze and iron while onlookers watch.

Decorative objects are for sale and we suggest you take a good look at some of the "seconds" offers. The Ta' Qali Craft Centre is located near to the Malta Aviation Museum and directly next to the Ta' Qali National Park.

Keep an eye out for the meticulous Maltese lace.

The Point Shopping Mall

Tigne Point,
Sliema, Malta
+356 2065 5550
http://www.thepointmalta.com

The Point, was designed by a well-known British architectural firm and boasts a high-end, sleek design. This is the newest and largest retail mall in Malta.

Admire the design and appreciate the expansive variety in the products and brands at the Point. In addition to stores, there are good restaurants, cafes, and special areas for children.

With opening hours from 9:30 a.m. to 7:30 p.m., shoppers have lots of flexibility.

Valletta Sunday Market

St. James Ditch
Valletta, Malta

This popular open-air market is held weekly starting in the early morning and closing around 12:00 - 1:00 p.m. Arrive early to avoid the crowds and to buy the best products.

Vendors sell souvenirs, clothes, DVDs, and traditional products like handmade tablecloths, crafts and antiques.

Practice your bargaining skills to get the best deals.

MALTA TOURIST GUIDE

Printed in Great Britain
by Amazon.co.uk, Ltd.,
Marston Gate.